Prolific Pulsations

by

The Authors

of

Prolific Pulse Press

Published by Prolific Pulse Press LLC

December 2023, Raleigh, North Carolina USA

ISBN Paperback 978-1-962374-08-8

ISBN eBook 978-1-962374-09-5

Edited by Richard Fireman

Table of Contents

Introduction

Welcome to the Prolific Pulsations anthology, featuring authors from Prolific Pulse Press. Together, we have showcased the chosen poetry and prose of each author.

With each of these writers, we posed questions about their writing life. We will present these questions first, followed by a barcode link for you to explore more, taking you to their book or other information about the specific writer. In addition, 2024 will see published works by several writers. This book also previews what's to come.

Feedback helps us to discover areas where we need to improve. It also helps us to know what is working for you, the reader. Please feel free to write reviews or contact us directly with your thoughts. Your support and the authors' dedication have brought us to where we are today. Everyone benefits from this situation, and we are grateful.

Steve Anc

Steve Anc is the son of Ajuzie Nwaorisa, a Nigerian-born poet. He is a poet with searching knowledge and deep meditation on universal themes, he is quite a modern poet in his adherence to language and his use of metaphors is soul-searching.

What would you like people to know about you?

I am a Nigerian poet and author of six poetry anthologies. I love poetry, magic, and the moon. I believe that every created soul is a star and I can testify to that.

What would you like people to know about your work?

I can't discuss my writing, because it may sound like self-praise, but I know that I have mastered the art of metaphor and I direct my work to the heart. Also, I can't list all my works here because I have written many poems; my works have been published by *Open Door, American University of Iraq, Sulaimani, Prolific Pulse Press LLC, Fine Lines, Poetrysoup, Goodlitcompany,*

Voice From The Void, Our Poetry Archive, I Become The Beast, Fire Magazine, South Broadway Press, Phoenix Z publishing, Western Voices Edition of Setu Mag, etc.

What is your writing process?

It has been gradual so far, and I have lots on hand as we speak; everything is going as planned.

Who or what influenced you to become a writer and/or who are your favorite authors?

I have wanted to be a writer since my teen years, but my passion for poetry started five years ago. My influencer is a Canadian-born poet, Robert William Service.

What are you working on now?

I am working on *The Fragments of my Mind* and *The Child Without Love.*" Both are anthologies of poems.

I am fine: don't read this poem

You don't have to see this:
You don't have to stress the eyes
Cos you won't understand
Yes!
You would not
You don't have to...
Nothing is wrong!
You don't have to read my poem
You will wither into my pain
Please don't read these lines
You could be caged.
Please don't go further
Tears may freely roll
Eyes may freely swell
Hearts may easily bleed
If you continue with this write
It may read the truth
Yes!
I said stop!
I have been accused
I have been depressed
I have been blamed
I have been chained
I have been bullied
Raped
Ignored
Used
Betrayed
Mostly for zero cause

I can feel your concern
Yes!
I can!
But you should not...
Life is funny
And I have seen it
You don't have to see that
You don't have to think that
Cos nothing is wrong
Do not worry
Do not think it
Do not stress it
I am fine
Forget the allegations
Forget the interrogations
Forget the accusation
I mean forget the...
I am fine
Nothing is wrong
Just let me be
I need to be alone
I need peace
I need rest
Please, leave me in the dark
I am fi...

A Tale by the man on the roadside

Set not your foot on the grave
till you hear what the gods are saying:
There is no joy in divided tracks.
The joy that dwells in envy had expired.
The morning had chased the mourning.
And the north pole and south pole are getting married.

"Set your foot on the right track," I said.
Seek the breeze and shrub of unity
with charitable time.
Wrap self with sublime sage.
Cos sometimes the heart speaks
the right thing for us to do.
Eyes thrust as confused tools
they see not what is right.
And it builds skies for misunderstanding.

Set not your foot on the grave
till you know that
life is too short to waste,
how to wear the critic bite with cynic bark,
and rightly un-wrong every wrong.

Please care not to trip the dead,
instead, rob the living with care and lively ornaments,
and only God will speed your Mark.

Joni Karen Caggiano

Joni Karen Caggiano is an internationally published author, poet, and photographer. She is a 2022 Pushcart Nominee for her poem, "Old News is Not Old News," published by *The Short of It Publishing.* She was privileged to write the Forward for the Best Seller, "I Am In Itself Poetry In The Dark," by the five-time Amazon Best Selling Author Michelle Ayon Navajas.

On *SpillWords Press* NYC, Joni won Publication of the Month in November 2022 and Co-Winner of Socialite of the Year 2023. Joni was a Co-Author of both #1 Amazon Bestselling books, *Hidden In Childhood* and *Wounds I Healed.* She is also in five additional Poetry Anthologies. Her first book of poetry, *One Petal at a Time*, will be released by Prolific Pulse Press, LLC in 2024, featuring Valencian artist Francisco Bravo Cabrera. Joni is also proud to be included in the upcoming Poetry Anthology, *A Safe and Brave Space*, published by Garden of Neuro Publishing, to be released in the Spring of 2024. She is currently a writer for *Hotel Masticadores.* Joni formerly contributed four combined pieces a month for one year to *Masticadores India* and *Masticadores USA.*

You can find a complete list of Joni's works at the-inner-child.com/publications. Joni's website is the-inner-child.com, Twitter is @theinnerchild1, and Instagram is @jonicaggiano. Joni is a retired nurse, ACOAs (Adult Children of Alcoholics) survivor, and environmental advocate.

What would you like people to know about you?

My alcoholic parents abused me, and the lack of parental care allowed other extended family members to do the same. As a result of that abuse, I became a poet and a songwriter at six. At seven I was singing original songs and was even on the radio. Thus, I'm an ACOA Poet, trying not only to raise awareness about abuse that accompanies alcoholism (or any dysfunctional compulsion) but also to interact with others with lovingkindness. I love nature and the beauty that God has blessed us with. I also believe it takes a lot of hard work to become a gifted poet, and one is never too old to learn.

What would you like people to know about your work?

I want people to recognize my name as a poet, and my unique style before I die. Seriously, it seems that many famous poets don't become recognized until after they have passed away, so if I'm going to become known for my poetry, I would like to be around to see it!

What is your writing process?

I utilize a word, beautiful illustration, artwork, or music, and I sit and focus until I have the beginning of an idea. The more I write, the better I like my work, and I have always been my worst critic. When I have a thought, especially in the early waking hours, I try to write it down in a workbook. My best work starts from two lines I may get as I lay in bed before anyone is up. Other times, if my phone is with me, I'll create a note on my phone because I get a feeling about something I see or hear.

Who or what influenced you to become a writer and/or who are your favorite authors?

I started writing poetry when I was very young to help cope with the dysfunctional chaos and abuse I endured. Oddly enough my mom, the source of much turmoil and abuse, encouraged me to continue writing. As I got older, she would buy me poetry books. Four of my favorite authors are Virginia Woolf, J.R.R. Tolkien, C.S. Lewis, and Ernest Hemingway.

What are you working on now?

In addition to continuing to read fellow poets and famous authors, I write short stories and prose. I am very proud and excited to have my first book of poetry, a dream I've had since I was seven, published by Prolific Pulse Press LLC!

I am currently involved in a weekly critique class led by Elliot Rubin, an excellent writer and poet. I am trying to improve my craft and am grateful for this opportunity.

Lockless

keyless is my lock, yet I surrender myself completely

thinning skin with shadows of whispers and prickling flesh

secrets buried beneath a stratum of my dried and crackling crust

my haunting heart hungers for a yielding stillness, I can trust

until my essence is so sweetly scented fading back into ash and dust

struggling to forget that remembrance resembling an unmarked grave

magical innocence lost in fall's carpet, golden and rust leaves, forgotten times

buried just beyond the massive willow oak of my youth and its crimes

colors mix with nature's caress and fresh air which carries me lovingly away

disquieting nightmares that swiftly strike their sword to diminish childhood play

for now, carved, a shelter delicate yet strong like an egg's armor where I feel

safe, as my breath is like a song which sends forth my overwhelming love

upon the wings of the sparrow or the red chested bleeding-heart dove coming safely here to cry, tears of dancing joy seen upon a child's face

yes, peace has beckoned and lightning-bugs circle sweet gardenias in a vase

where locks don't exist, fairies sing and angels stand guard in my magic place

Sundry Cages

seeking refuge, sorrows spill

like drops of vinegar

in respite, I lay them down

on hairy green leaves, gesturing

upon a trellis of jasmine white

buds' scent like heaven's gate

a lion sleeps still this night

gorillas' rough hands touch sadness

grooming air as I breathe

trees know my heart

prayers go up for me

the sins of the father

the sins of the mother

does my core rest redolent

of childhood innocence,

freedom from sundry cages

sorrow, regret, and grasping

all are guilty, so we raise

sluicing our own body's sin

florets spring from fingertips

melodiously I lay me down

hands of the earth kiss me

peace beckons

hope is a songbird's sound

Richard Fireman

Richard Fireman has been writing for over fifty years and has given readings at several libraries, Barnes & Noble, and several other places, including the Colts Neck Fair, in New Jersey, where he lives. He has also published numerous articles, both in local magazines and in chess publications and websites, such as the U.S. Chess Federation's Chess Life, chessvibes.com, and kasparovchess.com. In 2009 he contributed a chapter to the book Writing Away the Demons, a compendium of thirteen writers' stories of how each of them used their writing to cope with life crises, edited by poetry therapist Dr. Sherry Reiter.

In 2022 he published *Constellations* with Prolific Pulse Press LLC.

What would you like people to know about you?

I am a "stranger in a strange land" hopefully made slightly less strange by my poetry.

What would you like people to know about your work?

I try to combine my individual experience with my perception of the universal, so if
my poetry is successful, it will be a confluence of both and mean something to everyone.

What is your writing process?

I have no process; the words come forth and then I have to deal with them!

Who or what influenced you to become a writer and/or who are your favorite authors?

My freshman English teacher in college, Richard Leigh (R.I.P.). Poetry: Rilke, Blake, Novalis, Rimbaud, cummings, Eliot, Mandelstam, St.-John Perse; novelists: Joyce, Pynchon, Barth, Powers; short stories: Helprin, Shepard, Tiptree.

What are you working on now?

A second collection of poetry, tentatively titled *New Constellations.*

As Close As We Can Get

There is a pain in my chest. The stars
seem brighter. Thicker. Closer.

I walk with the dogs, I piss in the woods.
One smells a rabbit I saw run by, the other
something I cannot see or smell. I know
they live in a different world, one we cannot
inhabit, of smells we cannot know. I know
this is my dog's last year on earth,
last season his nose will know the ground,
taste the wind. Do the stars
seem closer to him now as well?

I cannot interpret his look except for the love
I see reflected in his eyes.
He walks more slowly now
but patiently, sure he will get to where I am
eventually. Time: I remember being half my age,
a world away, a crystal sky, wondering then
who I'd be now. And twice my age from now
will I be wiser or more foolish? Or just
more patient to arrive?

My dog senses I think too much, comes over,
licks my face. I cry. I would bring
the stars to him. We humans inhabit a world of love
gods can never know.

Unbound

The kite-flyer does not move
but soars, kisses the air,
makes vicarious love to the sun.

He stands patiently at the edge of the sky
unreeling his bound self,
sensing the shifts of the wind
like a blind lover,
and takes what shapes
emerge.

We are so far from God,
so near.

Sita Gaia

Sita Gaia (She/They) is a badass chronic illness warrior and TEDx Alumnae. She has had a chapbook published, *Knocking On The Body's Door* (Prolific Pulse Press, 2021). She has also been published in *Kissing Dynamite*, *Bitchin Kitch*, and *Anti Heroin Chic*, to name a few. She lives in Vancouver, BC, Canada, with her wife.

What would you like people to know about you?

I enjoy being challenged by other people on my poetry, as well as using poetry as a tool for teaching people about things that they may not have known before. I love how powerful poetry can be, and my poet friend in Germany has a line from one of her poems which I still remember from a year later.

On a personal note, I drink iced coffee year round, and have developed an interest
in gardening this year.

What would you like people to know about your work?

My work is meant to teach, and also to explore caveats about myself that I may not have known before. I enjoy writing pop culture poetry as well since I enjoy re-watching TV shows over and over. I am always open to trying new forms of poetry and love feedback from my writing community. I feel so grateful to have people in my community who see the world from a different lens and can offer suggestions to tighten up my work.

What is your writing process?

I often get words stuck in my head, and at the beginning I found it annoying. I consulted with another poet friend and she said she just uses those words to create a word bank with all of those words. My process also depends on my mood or energy levels. I enjoy using repetition sometimes because that expresses frustration for me.

Who or what influenced you to become a writer and/or who are your favorite authors?

My grade three teacher Jude Neale (who now has 11 books out), two of which were published with Ekphrastic Press (the "big dogs"!).

My favourite poets are Andrea Gibson, Ollie Schminkey, Rudy Francisco, Sabrina Benaim, Sabrina Demulder, Bree Bailey, Beck Anson, Nadine Hitchiner and Dane Lyn.

I am putting together a full-length manuscript on the Winter Solstice. Heather Pease helped me with this for my chapbook in 2020 and it got picked up the next year! I am very excited to have a full poetry book out in the world, which has been a dream of mine since I was eight.

I'll Have a Seizure With my Coffee on the Side

I love the coffee shop down the street.
The grinders,
how people hide behind their laptops
drowning out the world with their headphones-
whales under the sea don't care how far down they are.

The awe of how fast
the baristas punch in my order-
or how some of them have it memorized.
I like consistency.

It amazes me how they
can work while conversation
pours out of me like the coffee
they pour for their patrons.

How they smile at me
because they're friendly,
or just paid to do it,
I don't care.

Did you know that the coffee shop
is the best place
out in the world to have a seizure?
My seizures don't leave me staring
off in one direction.

One time I treated my Mum and I to a coffee,
& I felt the heavy pull
of fatigue from my meds,
collapsed to the ground.
After I 'came to', my mom
wiped up hot coffee from my chest,
using her favourite navy scarf.
What was my own name?

Where was I and why were people
Taking pictures of me?
The smell of coffee
reeked all over my body.

The floor was cold, clean,
but too hard to fall on, right?
Is any floor good to fall on?

No,
I fall without warning
and my head smacks the floor so hard,
I feel my skull move.

Metal Toilet

When I told my therapist
my life was better off
in pieces of ash,

he marched me out to my Dad's
car with strict instructions
to go to the emergency immediately.

I fumed like the exhaust
of the tailpipe on my grandpa's car,
before he died an honourable death.

I cavalierly texted
a few friends
about the attempt.

It was not for attention.
I had the perfect opportunity
the night before.

Smothered in love by parents
who were always home,
there was no good time.

Deemed unsafe in my own hands,
I spent the night
in the fluorescent dark.

When I used the
washroom,
I found the toilet was metal.

I kicked it so hard
with my blue Converse
low tops.

It was indestructible and steady
as a rock.
I couldn't even be trusted to use
a normal toilet.

Sometimes it's easier to
shut up about these things.

But that's not what
1-800-SUICIDE
told me.

Aariona Harris

Aariona Harris is currently studying English Literature full-time. She balances a full-time job and college while also finding time to write. Her passion is reading, especially classic literature. Writing provides her with a sense of belonging.

She has a passion for literature, just like other members of literary history. Her desire is to share this love with everyone.

Aariona has had her poetry published in various journals. The press has set the release date for Aariona's first book of poetry, *Loss X Mental Illness*, in

January 2024. This book is a product of a chaotic life. Every poem and word brought Aariona healing and acceptance.

What would you like people to know about you?

I'm a college student pursuing a law degree. My goal is to publish as many poetry books as possible amid that and pray that my work can help someone through the hard parts of their life. And if nothing else, be an escape as they work through it.

What would you like people to know about your work?

Writing heals my heart, my head. Most of the time, sitting down with a paper and pen or even a laptop saves me from myself. And maybe even saves me from the rest of the world!

What is your writing process?

Whenever I appear to get to the point of bursting with emotion, I sit and write each feeling that I can name down. I write why I think I'm feeling it, where it may have originated from, and what I can take away from it. I pick the most prominent emotions, and I focus on bringing the feeling to paper with a poem. That could mean extensive research, or just a quick search for better wording.

Who or what influenced you to become a writer and/or who are your favorite authors?

I'd like to say my mother influenced me to become a writer. But I think that can only be attributed to authors like Thomas Hardy, Charlotte Bronte, even a few renowned poets. I began reading their work very early, and quickly became obsessed with the idea of helping others escape into a new reality, just as these authors had done for me. Thomas Hardy will have to be the winner though, as I've gotten his work permanently etched onto me!

What are you working on now?

I'm trying to focus on poetry that brings happiness to the pages it is written on. Recently, I've started on a series of poems, I'm toying with titling it "I Think I'm Happy Now."

Un-Made

I wish to disappear

To erase my essence, as though I were never here

I crave the knowledge of nonexistence

To vanquish my involvement in this.

Dive into an abyss and drown there for an eternity

Unfeeling and disconnected, even from my family

Oblivious to the chaos that is the world

Ignorant of the biases which make it whirl

Utterly unburdened and in bliss.

I can taste the freedom of this

And I cannot help but to wish.

You

I am you

In the way that I love

Your favorite song

I'm a combination of your thoughts

Every part of me was made from you

Every part of you holds some truth

Some secret facet of information

Which holds in each piece

A sliver of my salvation

I am you

And you are me

Rebecca N. Herz

Rebecca N. Herz is the author of "Homecoming." Her individual poems can be found in *Sinister Wisdom Journal*, *The Last Leaves*, *The Madrigal*, *Prolific Pulse*, *Cobra Milk*, *Fine Lines*, and on *Medium*. Rebecca is a graduate student of social work at Rutgers University and lives in New Jersey with her wife and cats. You can follow Rebecca on linktr.ee/rebeccaherz

What would you like people to know about you?

Hi! My name is Rebecca Herz and I am excited to be part of this anthology with inspiring writers both emerging as established. During the academic year, I am an elementary school social worker for children with special needs, and, of course, a full-time creative! In January of 2023, I published my first book, *Homecoming*, with Prolific Pulse Press, which is dedicated to the magic of self-discovery and the power of finding one's true home.

What would you like people to know about your work?

The best way to describe my work is emotional, spiritual, and musical. I am drawn to the lyricism of poetry and like to experiment with different forms. Much of my inspiration comes from nature, music, and relationships past, present, and future. Recently, the death of my grandfather has led me to explore themes such as loss, grief, and mourning. Overall, my work is aimed at reaching people on a deeper level, helping my readers connect with their authenticity and find their voice.

What is your writing process?

I hope for something exciting and unexpected to come out of my likely long-term process with the new book, as I was pleasantly surprised by the outcome of my first book, Homecoming, which took me five years to write. I like to take my time on a new poem, with a heavy revision process and lots of drafts. I enjoy taking part in writers' groups with some amazing Prolific Pulse Press authors, while also branching out into new communities through open mics and workshops. I tend to experience long bouts of writer's block when I least expect it, which are most often broken when I least expect it. I run poetry workshops in my community which attracts people of all ages and walks of life.

Who or what influenced you to become a writer and/or who are your favorite authors?

I was inspired to become a writer because of female singer-songwriters like Joni Mitchell and Carol King. I remember listening to their CDs over and over again, and shortly after being exposed to these artists, I started writing poetry and songs. I would say I was a songwriter before I was a poet, though I do not experience much of a difference between my relationship with lyrics and poetry.

What are you working on now?

Now working on my second book, I have been exploring themes of heritage, ancestry, and connection to historic roots. The title is TBD but I look forward to watching it come to life, incorporating experiences and inspirations along the way. The poems I am submitting are part of this new collection.

A Single Flame

At first, it seemed the fire only burned for itself
the wax dripped to the table and formed little ponds
on which the shadows of that flame would dance
the singular spark of something inexplicable

not important really but for the singular reason
that it couldn't find another use for itself than to burn
the wick was there and so was the heat
the flame came on so naturally

that the object caught its purpose
so it is with all of us, we wait for fire
for something to ignite our souls
the wicks of our bodies

the wax of our love drips down
to form the material of stamps
for the letters we write one another
the shadows of what we mean dance

upon what we say
so on & on until
we figure out how to say it like we mean it
to seek the flame

in one another
we live to pass it on

the ferocity of the spirit
that lights up the world

each of us
one by one
ignites the other

until all flames dance in unison
over the still waters evermore

Brought Down to the Earth

Brought down to the earth, I return to my birth
come to nothing, foundered and yet
before my chastening, I would flicker as a Narcissus
from nectar to nectar, seeking
again and again my G-d's ambrosia
unhinged

Brought down to the earth, I find my roots
nested deep in the mycelium maze
strain to disentangle myself, alone
in the finality of dust, I scream and yet
it seems my G-d's
unfazed

Brought down to the earth, I accept my work
my solitude, abandoning
flight, at last
for the comfort of clay and wildflowers
for the certainty of decay, no longer
aloft

Brought down to the earth, we writhe
through the macrocosm, no direction, no
G-d, sheen and shadow determine
our plans to sustain and to survive
our only purpose
these days

Brought down to the earth, we seek G-d
in piles of dirt, which from our station
remind us of mountains
it seems collapse is our calling
so sprawled out over the humus we become
human

Brought down to the earth, we pull our nourishment
out of the dust that'll swallow us someday
without remorse, as we are, but
bodies merged into one substratum
for the coming
generations

Brought down to the earth, I cleave to my beloved
closer than I ever held the clouds
cocooned together, hanging by a thread
with our silken chrysalis camouflaged
by the forest's haze. We do
not hatch

Brought down to the earth, I am not myself
if not for her, for without her
what would I be?
Reaching, reaching, and then
alone, forced to succumb to the facts
of fallout

Brought down to the earth, the difference
between spirit and substance
becomes irrelevant
mere meanderings
of the mind, as now we are asked to face
our ruin

Brought down to the earth, by
the floods, the flames, the wars
I wish I were still captive among the stars
and chained to the moon
I yearn for my heart in Venus'
roseate cloud

Zaneta Varnado Johns

Zaneta Varnado Johns is an internationally recognized poet and author of *Poetic Forecast, After the Rainbow, What Matters Journal,* and *Encore.* She has co-authored collaborative books and co-edited two poetry anthologies. Johns was nominated for a Pushcart Prize in poetry. Her expressions appear in numerous literary publications. Her website is: ZanExpressions.com

What would you like people to know about you?

I am a native of Louisiana and have lived in Colorado since 1975. I am a poet and bestselling author. My best roles are wife, mother, grandmother, sister, aunt, and loyal friend. I love warm weather and nature. People, Colorado summers, tropics, long walks, sunsets, and rainbows are my best inspiration.

I am a premiere member of the Women Speakers Association (WSA). My poems are featured as the Dedication page in its collaborative book series, *Voices of the 21st Century* (2021, 2022, 2023). The poem "Caring Exchange" was the featured poem, to introduce the 2022 edition. I am an Editor of the *Fine Lines Journal,* now in its 32nd year. I serve as an Administrator for the Passion of Poetry, the Facebook platform for poets which has more than doubled its membership since I joined the team.

What would you like people to know about your work?

My life's purpose is to share light through my expressions. When I write about life's challenges, I offer hope to the reader. My goal is to inspire with grace. I know there is always someone who needs to hear what I'm sharing. My prayer is that my work will land in their hands.

What is your writing process?

My process is simple: I write (or edit) something every day. I can't settle down until I capture intense thoughts and feelings. Sometimes I pray for specific words to do justice when I'm writing a tribute poem. I write pen-to-paper although I'm embracing the Notes app on my phone. I type my poems and then edit. Sometimes I get it right the first time. Other times, I allow time and space for objectivity before revising.

Who or what influenced you to become a writer and/or who are your favorite authors?

Nikki Giovanni and Maya Angelou have had the most influence on my writing as a poet. I wrote my first poem after seeing Nikki Giovanni. Her feisty recital of her famous poem, "Ego Tripping," sparked my interest. Soon after, I was privileged to see Maya Angelou on campus as well. I am also a fan of Gwendolyn Brooks, Langston Hughes, Mary Oliver, Joy Harjo, Jericho Brown, and Amanda Gorman.

As for prose authors, I enjoy Michelle Obama, Nicholas Sparks, Terry McMillan, LaVryle Spencer, and so many others.

What are you working on now?

My *What Matters Journal* was released this summer. It was inspired by my Pushcart-nominated poem, "What Matters." It is a weekly guide for promoting compassion and empathy through mental wellness, self-care, gratitude, positivity, spiritual awareness, and mindfulness.

Encore, my third poetry collection, was released in September 2023. In addition, my two pending projects are a Haiku collaboration and a photography/poetry book collaboration, to be determined.

I am a contributing author in the Women Speakers Association's *Voices of the 21st Century: Women Empowered Through Passion and Purpose*, publication February 2024. I was commissioned to write the Dedication Poem for this book. Please stay tuned, as I am strategizing with WSA on how to bring more poetic voices into its membership and writing space.

Caring Exchange

(featured in After the Rainbow)

You enter a park lined with benches—
on each sits a woman who cares.
Imagine their hands extended toward you,
and their minds of subconscious prayers.

Imagine their hopes, imagine their dreams.
Conscious women are living full lives.
They are doctors, teachers, executives, and such,
business owners, writers, and wives.

One says, smiling, "Come, sit or stand.
I have lessons and stories to tell."
You sit by her and smile when she adds,
"Welcome, your presence is swell!"

She leans in and asks what is on your mind.
compassion is touching your soul.
You also have stories and lessons to share—
some secrets you have never told.

She says, "Take your time, dear Sister.
relax, I offer my time to you.
Share your secrets—share your stories.
The world needs to hear your truth."

You ponder her request to open your heart,
then you proceed to inquire about hers.
Both invitations are genuine because
a mutual exchange is preferred.

Together you trade stories of joy and pain
as you laugh and you cry out loud.
You stand taller when finished—your load is lighter.
You are emotionally and spiritually endowed!

My Walk Along the Ocean

Merrily I walk along the
ocean Majesty is mine
Fiery sun blankets
my back Pristine
waters at my right I
follow my
shadow—
my keen island
guide on this
bright sultry day

I absorb the ethereal
landscape path
sprawling with magic
I warily travel along the
lava— extrusive rocks
formed ages ago I heed
variations of
rugged black
texture Razor-
sharp
formations
command caution and praise

I am seduced by harsh grey
stones covered with lichen
Aromatic winds pervade my
body My spirit blooms—
one step closer to heavenly
bliss Tropic birds summon
me
I look up
Aloha consumes me
I exult with utmost gratitude

Jill Sharon Kimmelman

Jill Sharon Kimmelman is a two-time Pushcart Prize-nominee in Poetry. She regularly contributes to international themed anthologies and literary publications.

Her debut poetry/art book, "You Are The Poem," was released in November 2021.

She is working on her second book.

Jill lives in Delaware, USA with her husband Tim Little. She is the proud mother of her son Jordan.

What would you like people to know about you?

"I'm Dancing As Fast As I Can."

What would you like people to know about your work?

It is honest, sometimes raw, primarily fictional and always linked with love for my readers.

My poems are often written in a first-person narrator voice. This is done to allow my readers to identify more quickly with the story of the poem. I address issues of critical importance in my poetry, memoir-style poems, posing questions in open-ended poems to keep my readers interested and involved.

What is your writing process?

A quiet space, a blank screen, and me telling myself over and over, this is going to be my very best and it will be worth reading!

I leave it all on the page. Like a dancer, artist, or athlete, I give everything I have to each poem and make every effort to leave my readers fulfilled.

Who or what influenced you to become a writer and/or who are your favorite authors?

I discovered my love of writing and poetry by teaching myself to read a beautiful book of classic poems at the age of 4 years old. In all honesty I was probably drawn to the magnificent paintings that accompanied each poem. Nevertheless, I found myself enthralled. So began a lifelong passion for reading and writing. My mother, late grandmother, and my late father all encouraged my pursuit of reading, acting, directing, and writing.

My favorite authors and poets include Barbara Taylor Bradford, Jane Austen, Maya Angelou, Mark Twain, Louisa May Alcott, Geraldine Brooks, Kristin Hannah, Rumi, and Rupi Kaur.

What are you working on now?

I am currently involved in the translation of my first book, You Are The Poem, from English to Spanish and then into Hindi.

Also, a unique poetry/food project that combines my two all-time passions, cooking from the heart and poetry: a collaborative book of poetry, "Two Minds, One Heart," with my dearest sister-friend, MunMun Samanta, in India.

A Dirty Martini

Morning
displaced files, heaving stacks of mail
vermillion-kissed cigarette butts overflowing
square crystal ashtrays
everywhere scribbled-on-liquor-soaked-cocktail napkins

An avalanche of pink paper unanswered messages
atop yesterday's neat stack
what to do with all these THINGS
now that her heady scent was everywhere?

There was barely room for one martini glass
a deep delphinium blue with three olives
on a crystal stick

He had never known such a powerful thirst
words like slake and slay danced in his head
confusing him
mocking his efforts to offer himself to her

It was quite clear, she did not need his help

She had climbed atop his desk and here she perched
last night's laughing, tender, darling, irresistibly sleepy
"dance hall girl"
shredding the satin ribbons of her dancing shoes
and twirling the beads of amber and topaz that
decorated her chest

Perhaps, if he squinted, he might see her better
was she fair or dark?
a sleek cap of auburn hair with emerald green eyes
he thought her lovely, a pose of something distant
like a wish

She had not existed before the first martini
he drank the third martini from her shoe
draining every precious drop of gin from that
inviting blue glass
all the while, chanting her name over and over
whispering reverently the song of his
new mantra

What must he look like so early on this
the morning of his longest night?

He said her name again and again
it was a sing-song tonic that made him
cry out

He must find a way to keep her all to himself
he could write his name across her thigh
scribble a bit of a heart behind her knee
cover her in a fortress of liquor-soaked
scribbled-upon-cocktail napkins
an entire box gone to obliterate her presence
or keep her hidden beneath his desk

Now he wonders
'what shall I do, how do I begin,
one more time?'

Dancing in the Kitchen
(sixty years…together still)

They dance in the kitchen like movie stars from 1939

With her eyes closed, she imagines herself to be
this man's siren
all heady scents, fiery hair, throaty whispers
she could be a star of the silver screen
alabaster wrists, swan neck flashing emeralds and
rubies
the whisper of her caresses delivered by hands in
long satin gloves

With his eyes shut, he could be the UPS man
twenty five years old in summer shorts, flashing a
devil of a smile
his lips deliver a commanding brush of
sea-deep kisses that rock her from her toes
to her cerebellum and back again

There is music, a solo saxophone
drifting in through the open windows
soul-stirring on a cool and scented breeze

Icy cocktails are produced
as smooth as slipping skin, he removes her gloves
allowing her fingers to graze the rim of her
frosted glass, pluck a briny glistening olive
place it between his teeth

It's a shabby room
scuffed up floors, a patched screen door
counter-tops in avocado green

He washes, she dries
that's the way it's always been
sweet tea and ice cold beer to toast another
perfect sunset
as if he had arranged it all, just for her pleasure
his face crinkles with that funny lopsided smile
she knows so well

He fiddles with an old black radio
slow sweet jazz fills the kitchen, spilling into
every corner
crossing the room, he takes her hand

Sixty years of Saturday nights, still dancing in the
kitchen.

Kelli Lage

Kelli Lage is a poetry reader for Bracken Magazine and Best of the Net nominated poet. Lage's work has appeared in Stanchion Zine, Maudlin House, The Lumiere Review, Welter Journal, and elsewhere. Her haiku was displayed in an online gallery by Harvard University's Arnold Arboretum. Her published poetry books are *Early Cuts* and *I'm Glad We Did This*. She can be found on KelliLage.com

What would you like people to know about you?

In my heart, the things that make me content in this world are loving my husband, Ryan, being in nature, and teaching. That's all I need. I'm lucky to have those things and hope I'm remembered for how I loved and taught.

What would you like people to know about your work?

My work explores a wide variety of emotions and experiences. My first book, *Early Cuts*, looks trauma in the eyes, whereas, my PPP book, *I'm Glad We Did This*, remembers the light and joy found in childhood moments and lifelong friendships.

What is your writing process?

My writing process is scattered, a bit like me. I'll write down phrases and thoughts as they come to me. However, I won't form them into something until the moment feels right and inspiration hits my veins. I don't force my poetry. I let it flow as naturally as a spring.

Who or what influenced you to become a writer and/or who are your favorite authors?

I've written for as long as I can remember. As a child, I loved being able to create images in my head through storytelling; whether it was a flower or a frog, I loved to bring life into my words. I continued to do this on and off throughout my teenage years; then, I stopped writing for a while. After marrying my husband, Ryan, he encouraged me to tap back into this part of myself; he saw creativity within me. I'm so thankful for his belief in me, otherwise I never would have found myself again through writing.

What are you working on now?

I'm currently trying to find a home for my photography book. I'm also working on editing my second full-length poetry collection, which I will soon be ready to start submitting. I hope to explore a lot this summer and find inspiration from the world around me.

That Day on Sullivan Street

my father's car sailed down the faithful road / that cut
through our hometown / my ears buzzed with promise
of hearing my grandmother's voice / golden beams
outlined her maple tree, where the tire-swing sprung
roots / my scuffed shoes met her driveway / the blond
rim of sun turned crisp / edge of earth now buttered
and baked / my skin licked by butterscotch light /
without roaring clouds or chills pulled from the spine of
midnight / streams tapped on tin roofs / bold showers
mingled, diving into the center of sunshine / I found
daydreams could live in the same place as scraped
knees and dried tears / on eves when snow sticks in my
throat / I long to hear an ensemble of hazel eyes and
undented youth / I hold my palms out / feeling
horizon's surrendered river revival

Every Single Sport

I drew my thoughts into dusty ground
with sticky fingers.
Bruises above my eyelids
became purple and brown shaded makeup.
I pictured a gown to match.
The sun trickled out of peeled orange slices,
but no one else seemed to notice.
My ears did catch foul ball whistles,
daydreams claimed me.
I liked the way dribbles echoed
on a waxed gym floor.
Like a baseline of people from yesteryears
who I think I'd get along with.
Coach couldn't see the drums.
I'd slide on my knees to dive for wishes,
but nothing less.
Early morning dew dug at my shins
and clouds knocked the wind out of me.
I ran, but not with the team,
to another place where the grass knew what song
was in my head
before I even strummed it.

Kika Man

Kika Man 文詠玲 (they/them) is a writer from Belgium and Hong Kong. Kika writes about their mixed heritage, mental health, and travelling, about music and blueness. They are one of the founding members of Slam-T (a spoken word & slam poetry platform) and a PhD Student in Cultural Studies at the Chinese University of Hong Kong. They have been published in *Capsule Stories, Anti-Heroin Chic, Serotonin Poetry, Bridge,* and others. You can find Kika on X and Instagram @kikawinling and further on kikawinling.wordpress.com.

What would you like people to know about you?

Currently, I am focusing on my PhD at the Chinese University of Hong Kong with my research "Queering Zines across the Transpacific" (tentative title). Aside from this, I am trying to build towards a future in which I can teach, do research, and live through poetry. I do this by writing poetry on a regular basis, reading even more poetry (in as many languages as possible), and exchanging poems and feedback with many of my friends.

In an attempt to move away from the thick categorisation many are solidifying themselves in, I want to add that I am not half anything. I am both Belgian and Chinese (from Hong Kong with a whole asterisk on what Chinese means), I am genderqueer, trans, agender, asexual, and aromantic*.

*everything is romance; friendship is romantic and intense loving and caring.

What would you like people to know about your work?

Though I still write in English most of the time due to my location and network, I am trying to practice writing in my mother tongue, Dutch.

Similarly to 2020, when I told myself I would try to add more colours to my (black) wardrobe, I want to bring more variation to the themes I cover. I want to talk about blueness, sadness, and mourning, but I am trying to write more about my awe.

One time I told someone everything is blue and ended up painting with more colours. I still believe blueness can capture everything, but that does not mean we cannot allow for other shades and nuances to enter our lives.

What is your writing process?

When I write I am a "basher" (as Megan Falley has called it). I write and I edit, I backspace and change rhythm mid-sentence. I do not often "swoop," or maybe I do. Poetry for me is a way of processing and this often occurs in stream-of-consciousness exercises; I call this poetry. The moment I call my writing a poem, this changes and I will start minding whitespace, look up synonyms on Power Thesaurus, and play with wording.

Working together with many other poets has taught me to write drafts and to save earlier drafts. I also have my darlings' graveyard and many notes where I keep words, sentences, and other ideas.

I call poetry a way of living.

Who or what influenced you to become a writer and/or who are your favorite authors?

So much, so many.

The first poem I remember writing was for the funeral of my friend's parent when we were in third or fourth grade. The poem that I recall as my first exploration with poetry was at the end of primary school when I wrote a poem about fate and coincidence (if I am correct, they were having a dialogue). Skipping a few more years, I started reading fanfiction online and writing more in English. This transitioned into poetry very smoothly.

One poem I hold very dearly is "Hepple," by Joke van Leeuwen, a Dutch poet I remember from when I was still in kindergarten. The second poet or poem that impacted me is Paul Van Ostaijen, who wrote "Boem Paukeslag" (translation: Boom Kettledrum).

When I started writing poetry the way I do now, I was deeply influenced by poets Jesse Cale and Ashley Dun (the masterminds behind "Secret Midnight Poetry"), Savannah Brown, and other more classic authors. I have done my first Masters in Chinese Language and Culture and would like to also mention Li Bai from the Tang Dynasty and contemporary poet Mary Jean Chan. More honorary mentions go to my friends (Tove, Josefien, I see you) and Kae Tempest.

What are you working on now?

Definitely my PhD dissertation and everything that comes with it. A lot of poetry too! Dutch poetry, multilingual poetry, more Chinese poetry. Currently, I am running behind on KongPoWriMo (Hong Kong Poetry Writing Month, one poem a day in August). There are a few manuscripts up in the clouds and I write.

I just write.

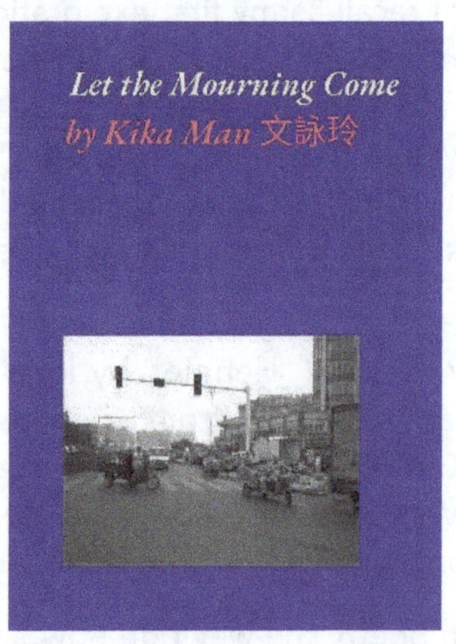

Rejecting your own body: an unrequited love poem

I love you to pieces, your nails,

and especially the dirt under them,

make my heart pump fast-

er than the bottles of kombucha

I finish in one day.

Cherry-thyme, mango-turmeric, grapes hopped.

When I see your body, it steals my lungs

as they fly away on a kite to heaven.

You make me want to live forever.

But every single time you reject me, I start crying

and then you are crying.

We're all howling and there are wolves

within us.

When you wear those glitters around your eyes,

I love how the thought of them lights up your face.

You don't ever need fairy lights, you are an elf

of a forest you're forever lost in.

Dance with me, you kind-hearted soul.

Please take my hands, my skull, take my brains,

I will gladly cut them open for you to dissect.

You may press on every nerve ending,

we are bruised and it's midnight already. How

will we spend the rest of the night?

Of our lives?

I would die for you.

I have already.

Took those pills, smashed them down my throat.

Did you feel my proximity?

It's the same as when we throw up with porcelain

only to ring the bell and ask for help.

I ask for you,

please, come closer.

Don't leave me

and don't ever tear yourself apart

at the seams where I have attempted to fix us.

When I touch your hair, it makes me smile.

The way you wake up, cocooned in blankets, makes me
want to stay at home

and make you an omelette of love so salty,

because I'll be crying over your softness.

You turn me flabbergasted, gobsmacked.

Did you really try to knock out my hope

for us to work?

Your sweetness turns my mouth to enzymes,

how can I ever stop wanting to knock you up

with some good old self-love.

Love me back, please.

I will never leave you.

Please.

How to make the weight of the world hurt a little less

Some days, the weight of the world

trashes around inside of me and stays hidden

in the smallest crooks of corridors cloaked in dust.

On one side of the world, it is raining people

who are clamping themselves onto aeroplanes.

In another corner, the fuel-drenched woods

burn their inhabitants alive,

making me think of the monks who would burn holes

in their arms in order to find enlightenment.

Can we really find the holiness of humanity

on this dried out plain

where people condemn so many families

to a whole solar eclipse of misery?

The moon tickles the ebb and flow

of water that will make even the most bedridden rise.

Horses will race us towards the end of the sunrise.

How can we make the weight of this world hurt just a little less?

Carrying the weight of the world in my tiny bed tangled up with blankets.

Ant-like construction works of plants in which I reside, a home made of fibre.

Love

is said

to spread like a petal

falling

on water.

It drops

and circles

around me, around itself.

The rain spreads love

like a wildfire gone wrong

and hopefully, maybe,

it will reach others.

Elizabeth O. Ogunmodede

Elizabeth O. Ogunmodede, a Nigerian national, authored a collection of short stories at the age of eight. She secured admission to high school by the time she was 10. In 2022, she was honored with a session scholarship by the C.A.C Grammar School's Old Student's Association of 1971/1976.

She has won honors on behalf of her school. In 2020, during the Corona Virus stay-at-home period, they published her collection of short stories *Lessons for Grandma* which was approved for seventh graders in Ondo State's secondary schools for the 2021-2023 academic sessions. She also published a poetry book, *I Love to Go To School* for elementary students. Her most recent book is *Ladder to The Top*, a young adult fiction written in two versions, one of which includes poetry.

What would you like people to know about you?

I am an award-winning poet who has contributed to several international anthologies. Online literary magazines and journals have published my works. Prolific Pulse Press LLC published my third book *Ladder to The Top*, a young adult fiction novella in the United States in June 2022.

I specialize in both product design and graphic design. My creative work includes animations, poetry, and trailer videos. I also love reading; the bliss and solace that is found in literature is my haven.

An online TV show, "Parrot Literary Corner," based in New York City, and featured in international poetry podcasts, has interviewed me. Kenya Times Newspaper and FUTA Radio in Nigeria have interviewed me, along with other online magazines. Channels Book Club at Channels Television featured me in a book reading session in Lagos State. Greenville and Hockessin Life Magazine featured me and my mentor, Jill Sharon Kimmelman, in an interview. *Blossoms Journal International*, based in the Philippines, also featured me.

I aspire to amaze the literary audience worldwide with my fifth book, a fantasy fiction novel.

What would you like people to know about your work?

As a teen author and poet, I write contemporary fiction that highlights societal norms and important values for today's children and teenagers. My poetry covers a wide range of topics, including family, literature, life, death, memories, and more.

What is your writing process?

Typically, my writing process follows this order:

Seeking/gaining inspiration; discovering the theme and most vital message of my work; figuring out the plot of my work and creating characters; discovering my proposed style of writing; working on my settings; seeking inspiration by reading works written by other authors; developing my book properly; and editing it. It is important to note that sometimes I write with the flow of my inspiration, rather than following a specific pre-planned outline to writing.

Who or what influenced you to become a writer and/or who are your favorite authors?

My writing influence was from several books which my father had introduced to me in my much younger days and those which I also read at school. I loved reading those books and they triggered creativity in me into becoming a writer.

Here is a list of my favorite authors:

FANTASY FICTION
Diana Wynne Jones
Brandon Mull
CONTEMPORARY FICTION/CHILDREN FICTION
Enid Blyton
Abigail Wild

SCIENCE FICTION
Arthur Conan Doyle

POETRY
Maya Angelou
Dylan Thomas

AFRICAN PROSE/DRAMA
Chinua Achebe
Wole Soyinka
Chimammanda Ngozi Adichie

What are you working on now?

I am presently writing a fantasy fiction novel titled
Halloween in Africa...Fantasy of the Realms, with which I
aim to thrill the world's literary audience.

Will Not Your Heart to Break

It goes beyond the bracelets,
beyond secret knocks
that opens doors for sleepovers.

It goes beyond tables for two
at some diner with pizzas too
the physical might just be a cover

It goes beyond shared tastes in flowers
beyond a shared delight in shopping
or that shared secret recipe for dessert

True friendship goes beyond them all
it seeks the entire heart of those
playing the game called "true friendship."

Know your friend so well
so you may stand a chance
of no heartbreak
when the chameleon called "friend"
attempts to shred your heart

Would You?

Some would never climb
the highest mountains
may never go a 360 degree
or cruise the deadliest jungles
for that one thing
their heart yearns for.

Can you walk through fire?
Would you take the burn,
for that one thing which you desire?

The journey of success
has two known paths,
the just and the unjust.

The just path,
I know to be rocky and difficult
The unjust,
quite easy as a pea
but what waits ahead
for the unjust men
who've cheated success
is deadlier than a visit from a nest of cobras.

Why not persevere
and take the burns,
climb the highest mountains,
to the top
in search of your desired success
for a just man you shall be,
free from the curse
that embraces
all cheats of success.

For someday soon,
you shall find that
which your heart desires
perseverance is key. Be sure to use it.

LaVan Robinson

LaVan Robinson is a 13-year veteran, he has written poetry since high school. "LaLa" is Robinson's poet name. He states that he loves poetry and will use it to inspire people and bring them closer to God. LaVan has several poetry collections available on Amazon as well as contributions to anthologies and literary journals. You can find LaLa performing at open mics and on podcasts. He can be found on Facebook, Instagram, and Twitter.

He has written several poetry books and his most recent publication with Prolific Pulse Press is *Hard Pressed*.

What would you like people to know about you?

What I would want others to know about me is that I'm a very optimistic person.

What would you like people to know about your work?

My work is written from the soul.

What is your writing process?

My writing process is that I use life as the backdrop of my writing.

Who or what influenced you to become a writer and/or who are your favorite authors?

I was influenced by the Harlem renaissance and Langston Hughes.

What are you working on now?

Currently I'm working on my short stories, plays and movie scripts.

Annihilation

White supremacy is vehemently on the rise. The participants are nothing but racist bigots now, not needing a hood or disguise. Boldly, they parade around, lashing out against other races and their long-standing foundation of democracy. They believe truly that they're superior, promoting foolish nonsense and hypocrisy. The leaders don't help the situation at all. Inciting notions that their country is slipping from their grip and the democracy must fall. Every race has a stake in the unifying of the citizens of this world and nation. Despite all we accomplish, it won't matter if we don't stop the free fall into total annihilation.

Blessings

Many people today rather choose to exist instead of to the fullest extent, living, selfishly taking what they can instead of giving the much-needed love and happiness back into this world and their fellow man. They complain when life doesn't go their way and to others, for their misfortune, they're to blame. They refuse to take responsibility for what they do, believing that they're slick and getting over, but there's nothing under the sun that's entirely new. Yes, you can attract the type of energy you put out. If this is the cause and effect of such, then there's no need to get frustrated and scream and shout. Things will get better when you learn this lesson. Trust God with all your heart and soul and no matter how you live life, be grateful for your blessings.

elliot m. rubin

elliot m rubin is an exciting american poet who has been in numerous anthologies and books of poems. His free verse style of writing is refreshing and easily understood.

to read more of the author's books of poetry, please check out this website: CreativeFiction.net

What would you like people to know about you?

I am still alive, they can enjoy my poems with that knowledge and look forward to many more to come. Also, my sense of humor, empathy, and humanity comes out in my writing.

What would you like people to know about your work?

I write in a style everyone can relate to and enjoy without looking up words in a dictionary or online to find meanings.

What is your writing process?

Keep it simple, try to use metaphors when appropriate, and if I hear a word, phrase, or situation which strikes my fancy, it becomes a poem.

Who or what influenced you to become a writer and/or who are your favorite authors?

I have two favorite authors, Charles Bukowski and Frank O'Hara. My father wrote prayers, short stories, and poetry, all of which I never read until after his death. Then I discovered three HUGE notebooks filled with his handwritten writings, which I edited and published in a book. I wrote the introduction and then kept writing. I first wrote crime novels, then switched to poetry, which I found gave me more satisfaction.

What are you working on now?

I have nine edited and completed books of poetry sitting in a folder on my computer, and I am still writing more. This year, I decided not to publish any more books except for those I already committed to and to submit my poems to paying literary magazines and websites.

chained to die

i was five when one sunday
my grandfather took me
to his scrapyard in brooklyn—
i stood on the sidewalk with him
in front of a chain-link fence
looking in at a big junkyard dog
who sat by a demolished car
with a heavy chain hung around his neck
as he stared back at me,
drooling

located next to
the kosher chicken slaughterer
i peeked in to see them
slice their necks, then stick them
upside down in a tin can

as we entered the junkyard
i held grandpa's hand tight;
he threw a treat on the ground
as we walked past the growling animal

years later,
i was told junkyard dogs
didn't live long
burglars wanted precious metals stored in the lot;
they threw poisonous meat
over the fence, then
waited to enter
as the dog
waited to die

finality

i see my grave
is already dug and waiting
wonder if god will dig me up
or do i remain worm food forever

as heaven passes overhead
    the living below
      will read my poems
they'll say

too bad for him
his stuff is good
wonder what he was like

as they turn the page

(from *Side Street Poems*-to be released in 2024)

Laura Stamps

Laura Stamps loves to play with words and create experimental forms for her fiction and prose poetry. She is the author of 49 novels, novellas, short story collections, and poetry books. Most recently: *It's All About the Ride: Cat Mania* (2021, Alien Buddha Press), *The Way Out: 40 Empowering Stories* (2022, Alien Buddha Press), and *Dog Dazed: A Novella* (2022, Kittyfeather Press). *Addicted to Dog Magazines: A Novella* (Impspired, 2023), *The Good Dog: A Novella* (Prolific Pulse Press, 2023). Her fiction and poetry have appeared in over 2000 magazines, anthologies, broadsides, and literary journals worldwide. She has won numerous awards, including the Muses Prize, and she is the recipient of a Pulitzer Prize nomination and 7 Pushcart Prize nominations. You can find her every day on Facebook (Laura Stamps).
Website: LauraStampsFiction.blogspot.com

What would you like people to know about you?

I'm a poet and novelist, who loves to play with words. I've been published for over 35 years with 51 novels, novellas, short story collections, chapbooks, broadsides, and poetry books from various publishers.

I'm also an avid gardener with 7 flower gardens. And I've been involved in feral cat rescue for 45 years. Lately, there are lots of dogs in my books, especially Chihuahuas and Yorkies, my two favorite breeds.

What would you like people to know about your work?

I write in a stream-of-consciousness style. At first glance this style of writing might seem chaotic. But it's how the subconscious strings thoughts together, which is why it makes perfect sense in the mind of the reader. And that fascinates me. I love writing in this style and pushing it as far as I can to see what's possible. It's the perfect style of writing for creating experimental forms and breaking the rules of traditional sentence structure, which I love to do. One reason I'm attracted to this style of writing is because I'm a huge fan of abstract art. Stream-of-consciousness writing is structured in the same way an artist paints an abstract painting. Gertrude Stein is famous for her stream-of-consciousness poems and stories. Virginia Woolf wrote an entire novel in this style ("The Waves"). The themes in my books may vary, but the underlying theme is always positive and empowering. That's because I'm a child abuse survivor, date rape survivor, attempted kidnapping survivor, and domestic abuse survivor. And I've experienced all the nasty stuff that goes along with that kind of trauma, like PTSD, anxiety, panic attacks, and depression. I've also experienced my share of stalkers and bad-news men in love relationships. That's why my books, no matter how humorous, are always empowering. I like to highlight the positive and offer hope to my readers. There's enough darkness in the world. I have no desire to add to it.

What is your writing process?

In poetry, I prefer prose poetry (350 words or less) or very short free verse poems (10 lines or less). In fiction, I prefer novels and novellas. I love the long form of a novel. It suits my temperament. It's easy for me to see the beginning and the end of a novel. That's all I need to write a new book. I absolutely love the process of writing a novel. The ride is such fun! That's probably due to the way I work. I write chapter by chapter. One finished chapter after another. When I reach the end of the novel, I go back and do one more edit to catch any typos I missed and to make sure each chapter flows smoothly into the next. Then off it goes to a publisher, and I start the next novel. I'm a storyteller, whether I'm working on a novel or a poem. I write both in the same stream-of-consciousness style. To me, there is little difference between my poetry and novels. All are written in the same style. All are narrative. In fact, I've published several novels-in-verse. My first draft process is the same for fiction or poetry. The main character introduces herself to me. She tells me her story or poem. I write it down. Then I edit like crazy (at least forty or fifty edits, more for a poem) until it's finished. If it's a novel, I follow her around month after month until her book is finished. By then the main character in my next novel has appeared and is anxious to tell her story. This is why I write every day of the year. New characters, poems, and novels are always appearing. I never take a break between novels or poetry collections. My characters won't let me.

Who or what influenced you to become a writer and/or who are your favorite authors?

That's an interesting story. I began my career as a fine artist (painter). When I was a senior in high school I

began selling my paintings at art festivals, and I
continued to do that for the next twelve years. After
college my paintings were selling in galleries across the
country. Prints of my paintings were published by my
fine art publisher in California (Haddad's Fine Arts, Inc.),
and they still sell worldwide in galleries, frame shops,
and chain stores like Bed, Bath, and Beyond, Target, K-
Mart, etc. Yet I was never completely satisfied as an
artist. Not 100%. Something was missing. But I didn't
know what it was. One day I bought a *Writer's Digest*
magazine at my local Waldenbooks. I read it cover to
cover. Loved every word in it! Especially Judson
Jerome's monthly poetry column. That column inspired
me to write a poem. It was awful. But for the first time I
was 100% satisfied creatively. Wow. That was the last
thing I expected. I always say that was the day my art
career ended. And it's true. I stopped painting, dug out
all my college English grammar textbooks, studied like
crazy, and ordered at least fifty books from the Writer's
Digest Book Club about how to write everything from
poetry to fiction to nonfiction. I read, studied, wrote
every day, submitted to countless magazines, and
eventually overcame my dyslexia. Yes, I am dyslexic. I
had always been told by my high school English
teachers that I had writing talent. And I was accepted in
all the honors classes in English literature In college.
But because of my dyslexia, I never considered writing
as a career. You can imagine how much the 2005
Pulitzer Prize nomination for my poetry book "The Year
of the Cat" meant to me, considering all the obstacles
I'd overcome in order to achieve it. As for my favorite
writers, they're all experimental. I love Anne Carson's
poetry books ("Autobiography of Red " and "Beauty of
the Husband" and many more). Every book of hers is
written and structured in a different style or form. She
is amazing. And, of course, there's Donald Barthelme.
Such an experimental goof! He always cracks me up.

The short stories of Ann Beattie and the flash fiction stories of Joyce Carol Oates were also early influences, and I still enjoy them. However, I would have to say Carson and Barthelme are my favorites. Always innovative. Always entertaining.

What are you working on now?

Earlier this month I finished a chapbook of 28 prose poems (*Postcards to Herself*) for a competition I was encouraged to enter. The last time I entered this poetry chapbook competition was 2004, and I was a Top Finalist. The main character in these prose poems is another hilarious, wacky woman, and I had a blast creating her. Of course there's a dog in this series of poems too. A Yorkie. It would be nice to win an award in this competition. But if not, another publisher has already expressed an interest in publishing this book. This week I finished a mini chapbook of 16 tiny free verse poems (*My Friend Tells Me She Wants A Dog*). Two publishers have expressed an interest in this one. And it is also out in another chapbook competition.

Excerpt from "The Good Dog"

88.

After work I stop by CVS. I'm out of shampoo. Oh, geez. They've rearranged the store. Again. Lovely. Why do they do that? Why? And where did they put the shampoo this time? It's not where it used to be. All I see are boxes and boxes of hair color. And no shampoo. And this. Tell me this. Why do all the models on hair color boxes look gorgeous? And why do they all have perfect hair? In the perfect color? Nobody has perfect hair. No one. Women know this. We all do. So why do they think they can fool us? I pick up one of the boxes. Wow. Okay. That's a beautiful shade of red. I put it back on the shelf. I have to confess. I've always wanted to be a redhead. Me. Secretly. Always. My secret. Mine. There's just something about red hair. You know? Not crimson red. Not ruby red. Not strawberry-pink (are you kidding me?). Just a nice shade of red. Like auburn. Or burgundy. Subtle. But pretty. Like the model on the cover of this box. Just like her. Wow. That's a gorgeous shade of red. Really. But how would It look? How? This color. On me. Wild and crazy. That's how. But, but, but. What if? I really love it. I do. What if? Okay. Why not? I grab the box, dash to the cash register, pay for it, and run outside. Into the rain. With no shampoo. Oh, geez. What have I done?

89.

"Is my hair too long?" I say to Walter. He's rolling
around on the bathroom rug, gnawing on a bully stick.
"It's too long. Isn't it? For this hair color. I think it is.
Possibly. I mean, I've never done this before. Colored
my hair. So I don't know. Is there enough dye in this
box for my hair? For waist-length hair? Like mine. Oh,
geez. What if there isn't? I could end up with weird hair.
Red on top and brown on the bottom. Or streaked hair.
Or worse. Ruined hair. Just what I need. Geez. This
could be awful. Horrible. A disaster. What am I doing? I
don't know!"

90.

Walter ignores me. No human can compete with a bully
stick.

91.

"Okay," I say. "How about this? I could cut my hair.
Possibly. Maybe. I'm considering it. Shoulder-length
hair. How would that look on me? Maybe I could even
cut bangs. Haven't had bangs since high school. What
do you think?" Walter continues to ignore me. Now he's
growling at his bully stick. Dog happiness. Totally. I
love seeing him like this. He's such a sweetie. My dog.
The best. I should buy that brand again for him. "Well,
it's not like I don't know how to do it," I say. "I do. I cut
my hair in high school. All the time. Bought a
haircutting book from my mother's mail order book
club. But that was fifteen years ago. Haven't cut my hair
since. I'm thinking waist-length hair is just too long. For
coloring. I'd need two boxes to do it. I bet. I would. But

I only bought one. So now what? I have no choice. If I want to color my hair, I'll have to cut it first. And if I want to reinvent myself, I should go all the way. Cut bangs too. Right? Why not? Or should I? I don't know. This could be a mistake. Awful. Horrible. What do you think?"

92.
Walter tosses his bully stick at my feet, pounces on it, and rolls over on my foot to finish his treat. "You're right," I say. "I'll do it. Thanks for the advice. You're so good at that."

William Waldorf

In addition to publishing *Sonnets and More,* Bill has been published in several writers' anthologies. "Each poem is like one of my children, making it difficult to choose one over another." His desire to keep poetry traditions usually requires a greater effort to rhyme. Poetry written in meter and rhyme has different challenges than free verse poetry. Bill lives with his wife in Hillsborough, N.J.

What would you like people to know about you?

I'm a Vietnam veteran, married for 58 years, and I have two children and two grandchildren. I held a C.F.P. designation, along with insurance licenses. I study poetry almost like an obsession.

What would you like people to know about your work?

I write in iambic pentameter and rhyme most of the time. My themes are lessons about life and the struggles to belong to be accepted.

What is your writing process?

I write two to three poems a week. I write it out in stream of consciousness and then review the work. The limitation of fourteen lines within a sonnet form can add more challenges to the work.

Who or what influenced you to become a writer and/or who are your favorite authors?

Elizabeth Barrett Brown's "How do I love you?" is my favorite sonnet. Wendell Berry's work can offer me peace; I stay focused on preserving nature with Wendell Berry. I plan to put together a chapbook, *Willy and Wendell Walk Where the Wild Things Play*.

What are you working on now?

I'm working on love relationships. How to know love and what to do about it, which brings out how to recognize abusive relationships and to avoid being locked in one. I always accept challenges that others avoid as being too hard, much to my chagrin.

Draw of Love

There are moments lovers of all ages
relish the attention, yet feel caution
deep within their hearts since being smitten
with hope. What will be their future chances?

Unable to be apart— absences
pull like magnets with enormous tension.
Not to be included or feel certain
will make most flinch as partners need glances.

They'll look in another's eyes to be sure
that their love's relationship will endure
no matter what obstacles encountered.
Together they'll never feel outnumbered.

With time the power of love grows stronger
as lovers find comfort with each other.

Unsatisfied breath

A woman's sigh is the ultimate high
whispered in your ear when wrapped in her arms
her soft thighs mesmerize as you succumb
to her lead, whatever she'll need to try

A gift or prize may make you agonize
with how to apprise love to your partner
careful to offer, to share, not smother
listen to those replies and visualize

more delicate than a porcelain vase
is a lover's heart hidden in its space
but a flash from a fiery eye may stir
a cautious lover toward carnal venture

to then welcome passion from another
when words bang the door of a deaf lover

(to be published in 2024)

Lindsay Soberano Wilson

Lindsay Soberano Wilson is the proud mother of three boys. She is a poet, and a high school English teacher. She is also the editor and creator of Put It To Rest, a mental health literary magazine, where writers put their personal stories to rest. Her chapbook, Casa de mi Corazón: A Travel Journal of Poetry and Memoir, explores how her sense of community, Canadian Jewish identity, and home have been shaped by travel. Her poems have appeared in *Fine Lines Literary Journal, FreshVoices, Embrace of Dawn, Poetry 365, PoetryPause, Quills Erotic Canadian Poetry Magazine, Canadian Woman Studies Journal, Fevers of the Mind,* and *Poetica Magazine.* She holds a MA (English) and a BEd from the University of Toronto, and a BA (Creative Writing and English) from Concordia University.

Follow her at: poetrymatters.medium.com

lindsay.soberano.wilson on Instagram

matters_poetry on X and Lindsaysoberano.com

What would you like people to know about you?

Although I'm highly educated in my craft, I would like others to know that I came into writing on my own terms as a lover of free verse, and support and believe in the power of the written word for people of various educational and cultural backgrounds. That is why I founded *Put It To Rest* for both writers and non-writers to use writing as a means of working through personal stories to put them to rest. Due to my flair and passion for wordplay, typography, confessional poetry, and allusions to pop, music, and art, much of my work has found a home in a variety of platforms both literary and mainstream.

What would you like people to know about your work?

My writing is honest and reflective, but it can be gritty and raw, as much as it can be heartfelt and grief-stricken. That's because much of my writing reflects my personality, which can be edgy, outspoken, and courageous, especially when defying gender roles or stereotypes about female sexuality. On the other hand, my soft and reflective tone is also featured in much of my work that explores mental health, overcoming childhood trauma, and facing the dark to find the light. Still, the most important thing about poetry to me is that it is accessible and relatable to the reader, resulting in my more colloquial and confessional tone.

What is your writing process?

My process is very organic but the truth is that poetry often writes itself first in my mind and sometimes the poem will write itself and come out on paper, and other times this idea buzzes around until I can detect it. But what I know for certain is that when life is more stressful or when I'm learning a new role such as when I become a new teacher or a new mom, my poetic writing dwindles, as it does for many writers when they're busy living life. So I try to take the highs and lows where they lead me and accept that sometimes I am in the observation and living phase needed to come out on the other side with more stories to tell. With that being said, in order to balance my organic style of writing, which often depends on inspiration, I have found that discipline, commitment, and goals help keep me on track.

Who or what influenced you to become a writer and/or who are your favorite authors?

The people in my life all had a part in me becoming a writer. From my mom who bought me diaries as a child, and took me to the library regularly, to teachers who took an interest in me, there have been many who inspired me. It was my grade 8 English teacher, Ms. Pitcairn, however, who awarded me the Most Improved in English award, that really changed my life and gave me the strength to follow my heart.

In addition, my *abuelo* Marcos Soberano, gave me a big, fat, red Merriam-Webster dictionary with a signed inscription for my 12th birthday, which also had a positive impact on me. Lastly, my father had a personal library that included some of the early poetry that I fell in love with, such as Khalil Gibran.

It's hard for me to identify a favourite author since I love so many different genres, time periods, and styles. I will say that, in my debut collection of poetry *Hoods of Motherhood,* my work alludes to influential poets such as Elizabeth Bishop and Walt Whitman; and also refers to feminist books I read as a student that left a lasting impression on me, such as *The Red Tent, The Women's Room, Little Girl Lost, Go Ask Alice, Alice in Wonderland,* and the young adult series *Megan the Klutz.*

What are you working on now?

I'm working on bringing my grandmother Toby Gornstein's Holocaust survivor testimony story to life. She was interviewed in 1996 by Felicia Carmelly, the author of *Across the Rivers of Memory,* about her experience in the same ghetto of Transnistria, as part of the series of recorded testimonies by The USC Shoah Foundation (founded by Steven Spielberg). So far, I'm in the process of having her testimony translated from German-Yiddish into English. I will be conducting research this summer, as I earned a scholarship for Canadian teachers from the Canadian Society of Yad Vashem in Jerusalem at Yad Vashem: The World Holocaust Remembrance Center.

The Eternal Child in the Mother

Now that I have this hood

I wonder when I will become
worthy enough to wear it as proudly

as a hood is worn at graduation

because there are passages:
dark passages in tunnels
there are no maps for

There are security checks:

foggy checkpoints through borders
there are no names for

There are scavenger hunts:

rigorous hunts on land
there are no rules for

This self-sacrifice is choking me
as though drowning
in this multiplying,
overflowing, mired
red-hooded gown
that keeps growing
like wild mushrooms
in *Alice in Wonderland*
or maybe
I should just *Go Ask Alice*

Because I'm treading water
so as to only take the air I need
to feed or be fed upon

before the next ebb and flow
of dizzying tasks

like *Megan the Klutz,*
I stumble, fumble, and my stomach rumbles

***

Now that I have this hood

I wonder when I will become
worthy enough to wear it as proudly

as a hood is worn at graduation

Because I'm still crafting
this mask that covers the face of my past

(Some days are faceless and nameless)

I made the strips of paper-mache
out of pages from memes, tabloids,
soap operas, cereal boxes, and magazines

from *The Red Tent, The Women's Room,
Mary Poppins,* and *Little Orphan Annie,*

Little House on the Prairie, and poetry

Tell me something...

Will this always feel like a mask

or will it eventually disintegrate
to melt and meld with my face

and become me:
the eternal child in the mother.

My Bubby Toby's Secret

She doted on me
and my smooth skin
warmly touched my hands

with her worn hands
dotted in wrinkles, sunspots
lifelines and piercing veins.

There was such ambivalence
in those tender moments
when I was warmed
like savouring apple cider
and yet afraid
of the cold expiry date
that her hands told me.

*(I knew by looking into her eyes
that she too
didn't know how to tell the time.)*

She didn't just hold
my hands lovingly
sometimes she would
pull at them
to beg and plead
like she needed me
to hear her
in a way my mother
wasn't able to
maybe because my mom
was too up close.

But I was more removed
from the crushing weight
of being the daughter
of Holocaust survivors
of knowing they just got off
by the skin of their teeth.

Though bubby Toby
didn't like to talk about *"it"*
she still told me about it
without telling me all about it
when she repeated
her mantra to me:

"to be a somebody."

Because nobody could take
that away from me
and how getting a good education
making your own living
and being able to rely on yourself
was everything.

Sometimes she hummed it
other times she mouthed it
but mostly she breathed it
and some days
she even said it
as though our lives
both depended on it—
like it was our little secret.

Wil Michael Wrenn

Wil Michael Wrenn was born in Charleston, MS, USA. He has traveled across the United States and resided in several places, but he currently lives in the hills of eastern Tallahatchie County, near Charleston which he considers home. He has a special feeling for the hills, hollows, and landscape of North Mississippi. He is especially fond of Enid Lake, which he considers to be one of the most beautiful, tranquil places he has ever seen. It has inspired many poems.

He has been writing since the age of twelve, first writing poems and then later lyrics and music. He bought a Sears guitar at age fifteen and taught himself to play it.

Since then he has written hundreds of poems and songs and had poems published in national and international anthologies and in magazines.

Wil Michael is a songwriter-member and publisher-member of the American Society of Composers, Authors, and Publishers (ASCAP), a national performing rights organization for songwriters and publishers. His music publishing company is called Autumn Fields Publications.

When not writing, playing music, singing, or teaching, he enjoys family and friends, reading good books, movies, travel, listening to good music, sports, spirituality, and just being out in nature.

What would you like people to know about you?

I have published three books of original poetry: *Songs of Solitude; Seasons of a Sojourner,* and *Enid Lake Mosaic,* the latter two books were published by Silver Bow Publishing, of British Columbia, Canada. *Fog* by Prolific Pulse Press LLC in 2023.

What would you like people to know about your work?

My work encompasses the varied experiences of life, and I want my work to touch people, to make them feel something.

What is your writing process?

I don't have a set process. I usually write from inspiration, and that can happen anywhere, any time.

Who or what influenced you to become a writer and/or who are your favorite authors?

I started writing because I felt I had something meaningful to say. My favorite poets are, broadly speaking, the British Romantic poets.

What are you working on now?

I have a new poetry manuscript ready for publication, entitled *Desiderium (Longing)*.

Reminiscence

The wind blows cold across the lake--

I think of you.

The chill seems to penetrate

straight to the very marrow

of my bones--

I remember you.

The crystal clear water,

like a giant mirror

lying on the surface of the earth,

reflects the slate blue sky above--

I picture you.

The trees catch the muted rays

of the sun...

The waves ripple...

The leaves rustle...

I divine your presence here--

wistfully.

The Death of Innocence

My father was a farmer
with a 10th grade education –
and a 150 IQ.
My mother was a housewife,
factory worker, and nurse's aide.

In the schools of today,
she would have been
a special education student
in math, although she was good
in language arts.

There was an innocence about my mother.
She believed in the right and the good.
She believed God would listen,
come to the rescue,
help and heal.

Bedridden and suffering intensely,
she asked God to do that.
And in her trusting innocence

she believed – as long as she could,
until she fell into semi-consciousness.

Was God there at the last?

Did she see or know?

Was she betrayed in her belief?

For me, these are questions

that will always remain.

All I know

is that I stood by feeling helpless,

praying, listening, waiting, wandering,

as I silently watched

the death of innocence.

Lisa Tomey-Zonneveld

Lisa Tomey-Zonneveld is the founder and manager of Prolific Pulse Press LLC and a widely published poet and writer. She is the editor of numerous anthologies and is an editor for *Fine Lines Literary Journal*. Tomey-Zonneveld is Poet Laureate Emeritus of Garden of Neuro Institute and resides in North Carolina.

Blog: ProlificPulse.blog

What would you like people to know about you?

Personally, I am a newlywed and a parent. My personal and professional loves tend to run together. Hobbies include creating art – mostly drawing and watercolor – writing essays and poetry, and fictional short stories. I also love swimming and the beach, art galleries, and gardens.

What would you like people to know about your work?

In some ways, poetry comes easily, initially. Once I get the rough draft down, it can take me a good while to get to the point where I am pleased. I tend to write backwards, so that the beginning comes last once I make all the changes. It's harder to get to the meat of a poem when you write this way; this is usually because the missing piece is the most crucial part of a poem.

What is your writing process?

Often I wake up with ideas brought on in the early morning hours. It is as if my muse wakes me up with thoughts. If I can recall these thoughts, I will jot them down and develop them. Since I conduct poetry workshops, I often get inspired by prompts at these events. I always keep a pen and notepad on me, as I may see something or think of something when I am out and about. I also use my camera as a source to help me remember moments I am experiencing. If I feel stuck, I turn on soft jazz or blues to keep my rhythm going.

Who or what influenced you to become a writer and/or who are your favorite authors?

My favorite author is the late Leo Buscaglia. His book, *The Way of the Bull*, has had a strong influence on my attitude. My favorite poets are Mary Oliver, Gwendolyn Brooks, Joy Harjo, Shel Silverstein, and many more.

What are you working on now?

When I am not publishing for others, I like to keep working on my own collection. I hope to publish an exclusive collection in 2024. I have more than enough poems to publish more than one book, but I want to hold off until I am happy with a collection. The other project I have succeeded with this year is the *Dear Heart* anthology, where art, poetry, letters, and photographs are incorporated into this anthology.

Cadence will be the 2024 anthology. We do a new anthology each year. The following are the anthologies, thus far.

New Publications are coming to 2024. *Cadence*, the anthology; Kaelen Felix's Illustrated book of poetry for families; returning authors with more beautiful collections, and more.

As a consultant with the Garden of Neuro Institute, I have been involved with the following anthologies:

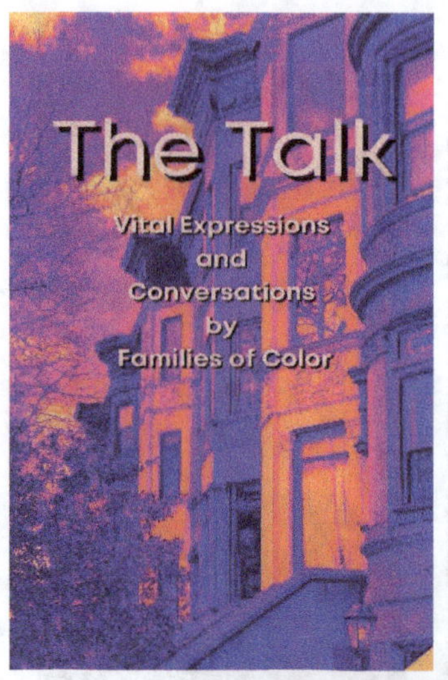

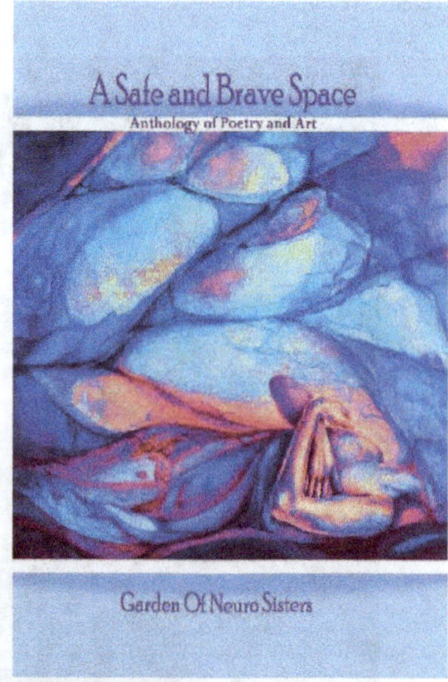

Poems by Lisa Tomey-Zonneveld

May I

As I see you crying

tissues are in my hands

shoulders are open

arms reach out

As you walk crumbled paths

my elbow I will offer

I'll fetch you a cane

Plants wither

new growth may or may not come

I can bring you flowers

apples, tea, ice cream

a kitten

perhaps a lullaby

a meditation

or I can sit in silence

here for you

whatever you need

I desire to be

your silver lining

May I?

Published in Fine Lines Literary Journal

Adjusting Lenses

humankind's nature

often means brisking each day

keeping steady pace

what happens when it changes

when the leaves of life falter

as the elder man

finds the keys don't play as well

hearing notes less clear

it's an evolvement of life

requiring tune ups often

when grandmothers cry

because their children are old

no longer in laps

still wanting for the snuggles

take them back to the time when

…

as life slows way down

keeping in mind the goodness

days when suns are high

looking to the skies for hope

seeing joyfulness each day

adjusting lenses

early in the children's lives

seeing and learning

each day is perfectly made

for any age to delight

from Silver Linings

Thank you for sharing in our joy of publication. This has been a fun celebration of beautiful poets and their works.

Your reviews are always appreciated.

A special thank you to all the contributors to this anthology. And for Richard Fireman for all his wonderful editing. It would have been a more difficult project without him.

Learn more about the poets, Prolific Pulse Press LLC by going to ProlificPulse.com